Other Kaplan Success with Words Books

Success with American Idioms
Success with Business Words
Success with Legal Words
Success with Medical Words

Other Kaplan Books

Access America's Guide to Studying in the U.S.A.
Kaplan/Newsweek Business School Admissions Adviser
Kaplan/Newsweek Graduate School Admissions Adviser
TOEFL
TOEIC

Success with
Words for the
TOEFL

By Lin Lougheed and the
Staff of Kaplan Educational Centers

Simon & Schuster

Kaplan Books
Published by Kaplan Educational Centers and Simon & Schuster
1230 Avenue of the Americas
New York, NY 10020

Project Editor: Julie Schmidt
Cover Design: Cheung Tai
Interior Page Design: Michael Shevlin
Production Editor: Maude Spekes
Desktop Publishing Manager: Michael Shevlin
Managing Editor: Brent Gallenberger
Executive Editor: Del Franz
Executive Director, International Products and Programs:
Marilyn J. Rymniak

Special thanks to Amy Arner Sgarro, Enid Burns, Jobim Rose, and
Pamela Vittorio

Manufactured in the United States of America
Published simultaneously in Canada

July 1998

10 9 8 7 6 5 4 3

Library of Congress Cataloging in Publication Data

Lougheed, Lin, 1946–
  Success with words for the TOEFL / by Lin Lougheed, and the
staff of Kaplan Educational Centers.
    p.   cm.
  ISBN 0-684-85401-5
  1. Test of English as a Foreign Language--Study guides.
2. English language--Textbooks for foreign speakers. 3. English
language--Examinations--Study guides. I. Kaplan Educational
Centers (Firm: New York, N.Y.) II. Title.
PE1128.L656 1998
428'.0076--dc21   98-29978
                                                   CIP

ISBN 0-684-85401-5

Table of Contents

How to Use this Book

If you've studied English, you know that after you've reached a certain level, you need to work on refining and improving your vocabulary. As you become more familiar with the English language, you want to be able to use and understand the same sophisticated, professional vocabulary as your American classmates or colleagues.

Success with Words for the TOEFL is an invaluable tool for student or professional nonnative speakers of English seeking to prepare for the TOEFL exam. It uses a variety of methods to help you to incorporate 450 words that you will be expected to know for the TOEFL into your vocabulary. Certain phrases vary in meaning according to the context in which they are used, and may appear in more than one chapter.

Each of the 30 chapters in this book focuses on words or phrases that are related to a particular theme, such as *Art* or *Economics*. Each chapter offers three different types of exercises that encourage you to contextualize and actively use these words or phrases. The first exercise consists of two columns in which 15 words or phrases listed in the left-hand column are to be matched with the correct definitions in the right-hand column. You should try to see how many phrases and meanings you can match up without using your dictionary. If this proves difficult, move on to the passages on the second page of the chapter and try reading them aloud to yourself or with a partner. The two conversations and the short talk you will find here use the terms from the matching list in relevant, realistic contexts. Seeing these phrases in their proper context should enable you to go back to the first exercise and match any terms that you were not able to figure out with their meanings.

On the third page of each chapter, there is a fill-in-the-blank exercise that tests your understanding of the 15 words and expressions covered in the chapter. In this exercise you will "recycle" your vocabulary by putting the phrases that you learned in the matching exercise and passages into sentences, contextualizing them further. This will aid you in retaining them as "learned" vocabulary. Be aware that these exercises occasionally ask you to provide the term in a different part of speech or tense than that which was used in the matching list—you may be expected to fill in a blank for the term *to major*, for example, with *majoring* or *majored*. This encourages you to develop and reinforce a sense of how the term is actively used in everyday English.

After you have completed the fill-in-the-blank exercise, you should review your work and check your answers in the answer keys on the fourth and final page of each chapter. Then read the conversations and short talk one more time to check your comprehension again.

You may work through these chapters in sequence, or by topic of interest. You can also look up unfamiliar words and phrases in the index and do the exercises that center around them. Whichever method you choose, you will master commonly used terms relevant to your chosen field of interest as you significantly improve your chances of getting a high score on the TOEFL exam.

Good luck and enjoy using this book!

1 Accounting

Match each word or phrase to its meaning:

1.	internship	to keep track of
2.	to major	planned undertaking
3.	to automate	basic
4.	firm	property of a person or company
5.	project	tiny
6.	across the country	transfers of goods, money, or information
7.	financial	school-related work experience, usually off campus
8.	to account for	report of facts
9.	fundamental	to do by machine
10.	transactions	responsible for
11.	minuscule	nationwide
12.	complex	partnership of two or more persons
13.	statement	dealing with money
14.	asset	complicated
15.	liable	to concentrate academic studies around a discipline

responsible.

Can you figure out the meanings of the italicized words in the following passages?

Conversation One:

URSULA: Are you going home this summer?

DAN: Actually, I applied for an *internship* and was accepted.

URSULA: Congratulations. That's great news.

Conversation Two:

DAN: Tell me more about your *internship*.

URSULA: I'm *majoring* in accounting. I'll be working at a big accounting *firm* downtown.

DAN: What will you be doing?

URSULA: I'm working on a *project* that will *automate* merchandise transactions for stores located *across the country*.

Short Talk:

Businesses need *financial* experts to help them *account for* the money coming in and going out. These experts are called accountants. Accounting classes teach the *fundamental* principles of recording financial *transactions*. This means identifying and entering all expenses, whether they are *minuscule* or *complex*, preparing timely *statements* regarding *assets* and *liabilities*, and analyzing the operating results of a business.

Fill in the blanks to complete the sentences:

16. Computers have helped to _____ many office functions.

17. No one knew we were _____ for product safety until we were sued.

18. The accountant reports to the _____ management staff.

19. The _____ transactions of accounting are taught in the first semester.

20. Every business has some accounting system to record their financial _____.

21. Even the most _____ error in entering the records can throw off the balance.

22. The huge new office building is home to many law _____ and other offices.

23. The _____ he's working on involves a lot of research.

24. Because they have stores across the country, their accounting system is _____, in order to account for the different states' taxes.

25. We have never been able to _____ where our money goes each month.

26. _____ give valuable work experience to students, although they do not generally pay very well.

27. He printed out a _____ that showed what we owed.

28. With her new computer program, she can keep track of the market value of the company's _____.

29. He _____ in finance because he wanted a job at an investment firm.

30. The computer network links all our offices, even those that are _____ from us.

Answer Key

1. school-related work experience, usually off campus
2. to concentrate studies in an academic discipline
3. to do by machine
4. partnership of two or more persons
5. planned undertaking
6. nationwide
7. dealing with money
8. to keep track of
9. basic
10. transfers of goods, money, or information
11. tiny
12. complicated
13. report of facts
14. property of a person or company
15. responsible for
16. automate
17. liable
18. financial
19. fundamental
20. transactions
21. miniscule
22. firms
23. project
24. complex
25. account for
26. internships
27. statement
28. assets
29. majored
30. across the country

2 Agriculture

Match each word or phrase to its meaning:

1. texture — relating to inheritance in a plant or animal

2. appearance — to make something

3. to tolerate — measurement of all the people in an area

4. to produce — to make larger

5. scale — one who displays special skill

6. to aim — decorative

7. to increase — to be able to endure

8. to protect — to defend against

9. to deteriorate — according to proportions

10. ornamental — to diminish

11. population — tactile characteristics

12. expert — to produce offspring

13. to deplete — to break down

14. to breed — the way something looks

15. genetics — to be directed toward

Can you figure out the meanings of the italicized words in the following passages?

Conversation One:

MR. MARSHALL: Today we went to look at different soils.

MS. THADWICK: How do you tell them apart?

MR. MARSHALL: Each soil has a unique composition, which affects its *texture* and *appearance.*

Conversation Two:

MS. THADWICK: I'm rushing to water my vegetable plot.

MR. MARSHALL: What vegetables are you growing?

MS. THADWICK: We are testing different varieties of tomatoes for heat *tolerance.*

Short Talk:

Agriculture, the science of *producing* crops and livestock on a large *scale, aims* to increase *production* and *protect* the land from *deterioration.* The main branches are agronomy, the science of crop production, and animal science, the study of livestock and dairy animals. Related fields of study include entomology, the science of insects; horticulture, the study of small-scale cultivation of fruits, vegetables, flowers, and *ornamental* plants; and plant pathology, the study of plant diseases. As the world's *population* increases, agriculture *experts* are concerned with producing enough food for everyone without *depleting* natural resources, or causing environmental degradation. Advances in increasing food production have traditionally come from plant *breeding,* but *genetics* and molecular biology will play a more important role in the future.

Fill in the blanks to complete the sentences:

16. Small-scale farmers try to _____ as much as they can from their limited areas.

17. _____ is providing answers as to why certain crops are inherently more resistant to disease than others.

18. Certain varieties of vegetables _____ insects and pests better than others.

19. Many fruiting vines _____ over time and have to be replanted.

20. Farmers try to _____ the yield of rice by fertilizing the rice crop heavily.

21. Animal scientists seek to balance feeding the livestock with _____ the ground from erosion.

22. To _____ new varieties of corn, scientists carefully choose the parent stock.

23. As the world's _____ increases, the pressure these new lives put on the environment is troubling.

24. When dairy cattle have problems producing milk, farmers will call in an _____ to provide advice.

25. The _____ of farms in the Midwest is immense.

26. Fruit growers are pleased to see the _____ of buds on their trees in the spring.

27. The _____ of breeding new plant varieties is to create plants that are disease and rot tolerant.

28. An entire year's crop can be rapidly _____ by an invasion of locusts.

29. Some soils have a rough _____ when you run your hand across them.

30. Because of the variety in color, shape, and fragrance, roses have great _____ value.

Answer Key

1. tactile characteristics
2. the way something looks
3. to be able to endure
4. to make
5. according to proportions
6. to be directed toward
7. to make larger
8. to defend against
9. to break down
10. decorative
11. measurement of all the people in an area
12. one who displays special skill
13. to diminish
14. to produce offspring
15. relating to inheritance in a plant or animal
16. produce
17. genetics
18. tolerate
19. deteriorate
20. increase
21. protecting
22. breed
23. population
24. expert
25. scale
26. appearance
27. aim
28. depleted
29. texture
30. ornamental

3 Architecture

Match each word or phrase to its meaning:

1. to derive
2. utilitarian
3. tutelage
4. sketch
5. intense
6. deadline
7. competition
8. jury
9. in place
10. to outgrow
11. to depend
12. to combine
13. practical
14. to gain
15. to render

capable of being put into use

existing

point when something is due

outside team that critiques work

to no longer need

contest among peers

to need something on a continual basis

to originate from

to add

emphasizing utility

to draw, to depict

preliminary drawing

to blend

individual instruction

to an extreme degree

Can you figure out the meanings of the italicized words in the following passages?

Conversation One:

QUENTIN: This summer, I'm *rendering* designs. I'm working on some new sketches. Do you want to see them?

GALINA: Thanks, but I'm actually more interested in *utilitarian* subjects like mechanic equipment.

Conversation Two:

QUENTIN: Architecture continues to increase in complexity. The client is now often a board, whose intentions and needs are not clear.

GALINA: And the *deadlines* are so strict now.

QUENTIN: Yes, the pressure gets really *intense* sometimes, especially when you *depend* on subcontractors to get the work done.

Short Talk:

The early American system of educating architects was heavily *derived* from the European tradition. A design problem was assigned to a student early in the term and was carefully developed under close *tutelage* from the master architect. The project, then and now, begins as a sketch, and ends in a charrette, a project produced on *deadline*. *Competition* was *intense* to get into the master-led programs. Drawings were evaluated by a *jury*, a system that is still *in place* today. Eventually, architecture schools *outgrew* their European dependence. Architecture training is now a *combination* of design, theory, and *practical* application *gained* in the studio.

Fill in the blanks to complete the sentences:

16. Architects study such _____ subjects as mechanical engineering.

17. All works are critiqued by _____ when they are done.

18. Architecture education _____ design with practical training.

19. When the _____ approaches, the intense drawing time is called the charrette.

20. The other students provide _____ to be creative during studio time.

21. He studied under the _____ of the master.

22. The jury system is still _____ to evaluate renderings.

23. Eventually, the American architecture schools _____ their European heritage and developed something better suited to their needs.

24. Architects _____ on subcontractors to help them complete projects on time.

25. Studio time is devoted to _____ rather than theoretical skills.

26. The pressure around a deadline can get very _____.

27. Architects _____ practical experience through internships.

28. The early American tradition _____ its format from the strong European tradition.

29. All final designs begin with a _____.

30. Architects can _____ the client's wishes into a sketch.

Answer Key

1. to originate from
2. capable of being put to use
3. individual instruction
4. preliminary drawing
5. to an extreme degree
6. point when something is due
7. contest among peers
8. outside team that critiques work
9. existing
10. to no longer need
11. to need something on a continual basis
12. to blend
13. emphasizing utility
14. to add
15. to draw, to depict

16. utilitarian
17. juries
18. combines
19. deadline
20. competition
21. tutelage
22. in place
23. outgrew
24. depend
25. practical
26. intense
27. gain
28. derived
29. sketch
30. render

4 Art

Match each word or phrase to its meaning:

1.	to demonstrate	items produced as a set
2.	studio	systematic procedures
3.	selection	responsive
4.	to expose	artist's work space
5.	styles	nonrepresentative; does not look realistic
6.	edition	to talk about with others
7.	movement	to subject to the influence of
8.	to discuss	to focus on
9.	methods	subject matter
10.	to concentrate	distinctive features of artistic expression
11.	abstract	execution of style
12.	material	to show
13.	sensitive	to add value
14.	manner	artistic trend unified by certain principles
15.	to enhance	a representative collection

Can you figure out the meanings of the italicized words in the following passages?

Conversation One:

ANTHONY: You were in the art studio until the middle of the night. Did you finish?

JOYCE: Almost. I'm working on some silk-screens. I need more *editions* of these prints for my portfolio.

ANTHONY: Your portfolio really *demonstrates* imagination.

Conversation Two:

ANTHONY: Our professor is covering all the major *movements* in art history. My favorite is the *abstract* period.

JOYCE: Really? I prefer it when you can tell what the art is supposed to represent. But I like how she relates the art world to broader social conditions of the time. It's interesting to see how the *styles* change so quickly.

Short Talk:

Art majors take a range of courses in art history, theory, and studio *exposure*. Students interested in art history analyze a *selection* of *styles* from various *movements* of the past, such as *abstract* art or impressionism, and *discuss* the *methods* of art historians. Students interested in studio art *concentrate* on ways to organize visual *material*, whether it be through drawing, painting, sculpting, or through use of another medium. Studio artists learn to use different tools in a *sensitive manner*. The enjoyment of art will *enhance* life long after college.

Fill in the blanks to complete the sentences:

16. Studying art can _____ a trip to the museum to see art.

17. The most famous _____ in art history were influenced by larger cultural conditions.

18. Her tendency to work in different media _____ the range of her interests.

19. In printmaking and silk-screening, students will use a range of tools and techniques to make _____ of prints.

20. Art history students _____ the significant topics of art.

21. Studio art time emphasizes the various _____ of expressing an idea through materials.

22. Even student artists can be very _____ to what they are trying to render.

23. _____ art does not attempt to portray its subjects realistically.

24. Hands-on _____ time is essential in developing your own distinctive style.

25. He studied many techniques and was able to use many of them in a capable _____.

26. Most students _____ on either history or studio art.

27. Artists organize visual _____ through a variety of different media, such as drawing or painting.

28. Even those students interested primarily in art history will _____ themselves to the art studio.

29. It's impossible to memorize every great painting, but as an art student, you will be expected to recognize a _____ of masterpieces.

30. Art history is concerned with influential painting _____ throughout history.

Answer Key

1. to show
2. artist's work space
3. a representative collection
4. to subject to the influence of
5. distinctive features of artistic expression
6. items produced as a set
7. artistic trend unified by certain principles
8. to talk about with others
9. systematic procedures
10. to focus on
11. nonrepresentative; does not look realistic
12. subject matter
13. responsive
14. execution of style
15. to add value

16. enhance
17. movements
18. demonstrates
19. editions
20. discuss
21. methods
22. sensitive
23. abstract
24. studio
25. manner
26. concentrate
27. materials
28. expose
29. selection
30. styles

5 Biology

Match each word or phrase to its meaning:

1. to bear   organic material
2. to dissect   to note similarities and differences
3. to compare   mostly
4. conservation   relating to nature
5. to acquaint   to organize
6. matter   the process of trying out new things
                         to gain knowledge
7. relationship   to endure
8. natural   to exert strong authority
9. to dominate   to cause to exist indefinitely
10. phenomena   to familiarize
11. to structure   to differentiate
12. to perpetuate   connection
13. to diversify   to cut apart for study
14. to experiment   natural occurrences
15. chiefly   protection

Can you figure out the meanings of the italicized words in the following passages?

Conversation One:

HARRY: I wasn't sure if I could *bear* the *dissection* part of the anatomy class.

ELIZABETH: That's the only way to really *compare* the organ systems.

HARRY: I guess I'll never be a good doctor unless I can survive anatomy.

Conversation Two:

ELIZABETH: I saw you out on the college's boat.

HARRY: That was for my marine ecosystems class. The professor is *chiefly* interested in *conservation* of natural habitats.

ELIZABETH: Learning how to preserve the natural history right around campus must be fun.

Short Talk:

Biology *acquaints* student with the nature of living *matter* and explains the *relationships* between different parts of the *natural* world. Contemporary biology is centered around three *dominant* principles: ecology, physiology, and genetics. Most programs emphasize applying biological *phenomena* to everyday life. Classes will discuss how cells are *structured* and how they function, the physiology of plants, and how all life *perpetuates* and *diversifies* itself through the evolutionary process. Biology students also have laboratory time, which emphasizes *experimentation*.

Fill in the blanks to complete the sentences:

16. He is _____ interested in the various orchid species.

17. Plants and animals find ways to _____ themselves and carry on to the next generation.

18. There are regional and global _____ problems as habitats get harder to manage.

19. The learning process of using _____ in the laboratory is a cornerstone of the discipline of biology.

20. Students can begin to _____ themselves to the wide range of living things in a biology class.

21. Environmental biology topics include discussions of the diversity in the _____ world.

22. Genetics is so fundamental to all life that it _____ the study of biology.

23. For the uninitiated student, the nauseating sights and smells of the anatomy lab can be hard to _____.

24. Evolution has allowed plants and animals to _____ to best suit their individual environments.

25. The laboratory part of the biology class teaches students methods by which to describe natural _____.

26. A class in applied ecology looks at the _____ between humans and their environment.

27. With a microscope, you can see how cells are _____.

28. An anatomy class will compare the development of different vertebrate classes through _____ and study of animal models.

29. Biologists study living _____ from a variety of species and habitats.

30. Students will _____ the various functions of plants in a botany class.

Answer Key

1. to endure
2. to cut apart for study
3. to note similarities and differences
4. protection
5. to familiarize
6. organic material
7. connection
8. relating to nature
9. to exert strong authority
10. natural occurrences
11. to organize
12. to cause to exist indefinitely
13. to differentiate
14. the process of trying out new things to gain knowledge
15. mostly

16. chiefly
17. perpetuate
18. conservation
19. experiments
20. acquaint
21. natural
22. dominates
23. bear
24. diversify
25. phenomena
26. relationship
27. structured
28. dissection
29. matter
30. compare

6 Chemistry

Match each word or phrase to its meaning:

1. to terrify	10 amount, relative position
2. to tailor	5 principal
3. to collaborate	2 blending
4. original	9 power, capacity
5. lead	14 response
6. author	6 writer
7. conference	13 group
8. comprehensive	1 to frighten
9. energy	12 guidelines
10. level	3 to work productively with
11. example	7 a meeting to discuss matters of common concern
12. principles	11 something that serves as a pattern
13. set	15 to make specific to
14. reaction	8 overarching
15. synthesis	4 source

Can you figure out the meanings of the italicized words in the following passages?

Conversation One:

RAVI: I'm taking an independent study class in chemistry this year.

SONAL: Being alone in class sounds *terrifying*. ~~big thirteen~~

RAVI: No, not really. It's great because everything is *tailored* to my interests.

Conversation Two:

SONAL: I'm *collaborating* with one of my faculty members on an original paper. It's about the *synthesis* of magnesium and carbon compounds.

RAVI: Are you the principal *author*?

SONAL: No. My mentor is the *lead* author.

RAVI: I hope you get to go to the *conference* to deliver the presentation. It would be kind of upsetting if the paper got a lot of publicity and you weren't able to benefit from it.

Short Talk:

Chemistry provides a *comprehensive* description of the interaction of matter and *energy* at the atomic level. *Examples* are drawn from research, together with theoretical *principles*, and are used to examine a diverse *set* of subjects, such as structure, processes, *reactions*, and *synthesis* of compounds. Chemists often *collaborate* on experiments and academic papers.

Fill in the blanks to complete the sentences:

16. Lucky students can _____ with a professor to create a presentation.

17. The senior researcher on the paper is the _____ author.

18. Having the teacher's undivided attention can _____ some students.

19. Atoms emit _____.

20. The blending of different chemicals led to an interesting _____ in the lab.

21. The chemicals are grouped into a logical _____.

22. An independent study course is a great opportunity _____ the content to your individual interests and needs.

23. He made a highly detailed and _____ assessment of the department's program.

24. The fundamental _____ of chemistry are repeated in the more advanced classes.

25. Academic scholars gather at _____ to discuss trends in their field.

26. Research needs to be _____ in order to generate much interest.

27. The _____ of energy at which atoms exist can be measured.

28. Most likely, your professor will be the _____ of many papers and will have much to teach you about research.

29. The chemicals had a vigorous _____ to the introduction of new material.

30. In addition to the work from the textbook, she requires her students to find _____ in the news of how chemistry affects our everyday lives.

Answer Key

1. to frighten
2. to make specific to
3. to work productively with
4. source
5. principal
6. writer
7. a meeting to discuss matters of common concern
8. overarching
9. power, capacity
10. amount, relative position
11. something that illustrates a pattern
12. guidelines
13. group
14. response
15. blending
16. collaborate
17. lead
18. terrify
19. energy
20. synthesis
21. set
22. to tailor
23. comprehensive
24. principles
25. conferences
26. original
27. level
28. author
29. reaction
30. examples

7 Communications

Match each word or phrase to its meaning:

1. message — ₆ fast
2. paradigm — to exclude others
3. to intimidate — a subdivision
4. to restrict — to spread throughout
5. revolution — ₁₀ period of ten years
6. rapid — ₁₅ important
7. digital — to make timid
8. central — ₁₁ core
9. discourse — to meet
10. decade — ₁ communication
11. sector — ₁₂ highly refined
12. sophisticated — conversation
13. to permeate — massive change
14. to converge — ₇ using numerical digits or numbers to represent all variables in a problem
15. crucial — archetype

Can you figure out the meaning of the italicized words in the following passages?

Conversation One:

MONICA: Our class is looking at cultural *messages* sent via film, the news, and the Internet.

JAMES: Our professor says that these tools are creating new *paradigms* for teaching and learning.

MONICA: I am *intimidated* by global communication via the Internet.

Conversation Two:

MONICA: My project is on the use of color on Internet sites.

JAMES: Is the color used there any different?

MONICA: The range is somewhat *restricted* compared to other media.

JAMES: Are people responding to it in the same way?

Short Talk:

The information and media *revolution* is *rapidly* changing economic, political, social, and cultural realities around the world. *Digital* media, information technology, and the Internet have become *central* to culture, communication, and social *discourse* as well as global business and politics. Before this *decade*, information technology was considered an independent *sector* requiring *sophisticated* expertise. Now this technology *permeates* through every aspect of society. Understanding the *converging* technical, economic, social, and political aspect of the global communications environment is *crucial*.

Fill in the blanks to complete the sentences:

16. Copyright protection still _____ the use of material found on the Internet.

17. Interactiveness is _____ to the Internet.

18. It is _____ to have leadership in communications technology.

19. The rapid changes in communication technology qualify it as a _____.

20. The Internet created a new way to send cultural _____ to others.

21. E-mail has created a new time paradigm in social _____.

22. The Internet has created a new _____ through which to get information.

23. No _____ of society has been left untouched by the boom in telecommunications.

24. People who have not tried the latest technology are likely to be _____ by it.

25. Electronic and computer-mediated communications have _____ through society all the way down to the personal user.

26. Media, computing, and telecommunications are _____ around global communications.

27. The changes came about very _____—almost overnight.

28. _____ technology is more effective than other technology in the handling of data and mathematical problems.

29. Because the Internet cuts through so many facets of society, _____ applications of the technology are necessary.

30. In just a couple of _____, the number of Web sites on the Internet grew from very few to millions.

Answer Key

1. communication
2. archetype
3. to make timid
4. to exclude others
5. massive change
6. fast
7. using numerical digits or numbers to represent all variables in a problem
8. core
9. conversation
10. period of ten years
11. subdivision
12. highly refined
13. to spread throughout
14. to meet
15. important
16. restricts
17. central
18. crucial
19. revolution
20. messages
21. discourse
22. paradigm
23. sector
24. intimidated
25. permeated
26. converging
27. rapidly
28. digital
29. sophisticated
30. decades

Match each word or phrase to its meaning:

1. to define	to handle or work with
2. to describe	easily accessible
3. assignment	to provide with a set of instructions
4. essential	task or problem-solving exercise
5. to rely	to have a solid knowledge of
6. to manipulate	to find solutions to
7. to program	to win through effort
8. steps	generalized procedures
9. to solve	to specify or delineate
10. to provide	stages in a process
11. to capture	exacting
12. fluent	necessary
13. guidelines	to furnish or supply
14. available	to give an account of
15. precise	to depend

Can you figure out the meaning of the italicized words in the following passages?

Conversation One:

PAULA: How far did you get with the computer program?

ABDUL: I am still trying to *define* the *steps* we should follow.

PAULA: I managed to write a *description* of the problem to be *solved*.

Conversation Two:

PAULA: I'm trying to apply a new *programming* technique to an *assignment*.

ABDUL: What language are you using?

PAULA: We're studying BASIC in this class. I'm almost *fluent* in it already.

Short Talk:

Computers are an *essential* part of any work, and increasingly home, environment. Computers *rely* on *programs* to *manipulate* information. Learning to create computer programs is a chance to use analytic skills to *solve* problems. Students taking a computer programming class will learn to define a problem and *precisely* define the *steps* to solve the problem. The computer program *provides* a structure for *capturing* and using information. Students will become *fluent* in the rules and *guidelines* of programming, and learn to use the different computer languages *available*.

Fill in the blanks to complete the sentences:

16. Programmers have to define the _____ to be followed in solving a problem.

17. Class _____ encourage students to work in small groups to solve a problem.

18. The steps for solving a problem must be stated _____.

19. Often a programmer can _____ charts or graphs to illustrate the information process.

20. Every office _____ on computers to store and manipulate information.

21. There are many computer programming languages _____ on the market.

22. It is often difficult to _____ in words the steps a program must take to solve an information problem.

23. She is _____ in more than one computer language, which gives her job flexibility.

24. It is _____ that computer programs respond to the information needs of an office.

25. Information in the computer program can be _____ in different ways to meet different information needs.

26. Computer programmers implement _____ to information needs.

27. While there are _____ for programming in a language, each programmer has his or her own style.

28. Computer programmers can help users _____ the nature of the problem.

29. _____ for computers is a skill that opens career opportunities.

30. _____ data is not enough—companies want to be able to use it as well.

Answer Key

1. to specify or delineate
2. to give an account of
3. task or exercise
4. necessary
5. to depend
6. to handle or work with
7. to provide with a set of instructions
8. stages in a process
9. to find solutions to
10. to furnish or supply
11. to win through effort
12. having a solid knowledge of
13. generalized procedures
14. easily accessible
15. exacting

16. steps
17. assignments
18. precisely
19. provide
20. relies
21. available
22. describe
23. fluent
24. essential
25. manipulated
26. solutions
27. guidelines
28. define
29. programming
30. capturing

9 Design

Match each word or phrase to its meaning:

1. hands-on   basis for growth
2. to complete   to associate or link together
3. proficiency   to make known
4. portfolio   someone who acquires goods
5. to connect   firm that makes reproductive work
6. tactic   skill
7. consumer   tangible visual representation
8. foundation   to complete or bring to perfection
9. visual   to advance
10. to complement   direct, active participation
11. printer   to bring onto the market
12. to convey   collected materials representing a person's work
13. to further   relating to the sense of sight
14. image   to finish
15. launch   a strategy for achieving a goal

Can you figure out the meanings of the italicized words in the following passages?

Conversation One:

ROY: This semester's design class is great. It uses a very *hands-on* approach in which we complete several projects.

CARRIE: We're becoming *proficient* in techniques that we can use in a job later on.

ROY: I'll put these projects in my *portfolio* of work.

Conversation Two:

CARRIE: The field trip to the *printing* plant was interesting. Now I can *connect* the creative part of what I do with the technology that produces the finished job.

CARRIE: Next month's field trip to the advertising agency looks valuable.

ROY: I want to learn more about the different *tactics* professionals use to *launch* a new product to consumers.

Short Talk:

A class in graphic design provides a good *foundation* for a career in *visual* communication. Designers use type, color, and shapes to *complement* the written word in order to *convey* a message. Designers must work to keep the visual *image* clear and legible. They must also make sure the work can be produced by a *printer* or other manufacturer within the client's budget and time frame. Completing sample projects in class *furthers* the understanding of the design process.

Fill in the blanks to complete the sentences:

16. Before you _____ your first design project, you will learn several principles of visual communication.

17. Advertising and marketing use a number of _____ to inform the public about an idea or product.

18. Good design should _____ a message.

19. Designers assemble various visual _____ to promote a product or invite a reader to learn more about something.

20. Layout programs on the computer allow for more people to have a direct, _____ learning experience in design.

21. Designers make sure the words and the graphics _____ each other to convey a powerful message.

22. Having some class project in your _____ of samples will impress someone who interviews you for a job.

23. Class work in design is a good _____ for getting a job as a graphic designer.

24. _____ communication can reach consumers through a variety of formats, including print and television.

25. A designer has to set up the design so that a _____ can produce the job.

26. Whether or not they know it, _____ are influenced by visual communication to try a product.

27. Student designers can _____ their skills by finding an internship that gives them more experience.

28. Students gain _____ in techniques that will serve them well in their future endeavors.

29. New product _____ use attention-grabbing tactics to attract consumers.

30. Designers _____ words to the look to convey a message to the viewer.

Answer Key

1. direct, active participation
2. to finish
3. skill
4. collected materials representing a person's work
5. to associate or to link together
6. strategy for achieving a goal
7. someone who acquires goods
8. basis for growth
9. relating to the sense of sight
10. to complete or bring to perfection
11. firm that makes reproductive work
12. to make known
13. to advance
14. tangible visual representation
15. to bring onto the market
16. complete
17. tactics
18. convey
19. images
20. hands-on
21. complement
22. portfolio
23. foundation
24. visual
25. printer
26. consumers
27. further
28. proficiency
29. launches
30. connect

10 Ecology

Match each word or phrase to its meaning:

1. organism — to live in
2. distressing — effect
3. negative — speech
4. impact — to give form to
5. eye-opening — striking *(llmctivo).*
6. deceptive *(en ynov)* — to take part in
7. impressive — an integrated community of living organisms
8. ecosystem — any form of life
9. physical — group that interacts with another group in a specific area
10. to shape — bad
11. aquatic — material characteristics
12. community — living in or near the water
13. lecture — awareness-raising
14. to participate — troubling
15. to inhabit — misleading *errones*
    habitgr –   *desonientidr*

Can you figure out the meanings of the italicized words in the following passages?

Conversation One:

BARBARA: I had no idea so many *organisms* lived in a river.

LEE: It's really *distressing* to learn about the *negative impact* of pollution on rivers and lakes.

BARBARA: You're so right about that.

Conversation Two:

LEE: After our outing today, I'm much more aware of the different characteristics of water.

BARBARA: Yes, the field trips for this class have been an *eye-opening* experience.

LEE: On the surface, the river and lakes look *deceptively* simple.

BARBARA: The teacher's knowledge of *aquatic* life is *impressive*. She really got into detail when she was describing the Great Lake *ecosystem*.

Short Talk:

Lakes, rivers, and wetlands are all part of the freshwater *ecosystem*. A class on this topic would cover the *physical* characteristics of freshwater habitats and how they *shape* the *aquatic communities* that live in them, which include *organisms* like water lilies, minnows, and ducks. Through *lectures* and field trips, *participants* will become familiar with different freshwater ecosystems and the organisms that *inhabit* them.

Fill in the blanks to complete the sentences:

16. The physical environment _____ and influences the kind of organisms that live in it.

17. The calm surface of the water is _____, as the life under the surface is very active.

18. The human _____ on an ecosystem is often irreversible.

19. Aquatic organisms and plants interact in an underwater _____.

20. A large number of plants and animals _____ the world beneath the water's surface.

21. After taking a class in ecology of freshwater systems, you will be better able to see the _____ characteristics of a freshwater ecosystem.

22. Her lecture on the number and variety of freshwater organisms was _____ in its detail and professionalism.

23. Classes can find ways _____ in the ecosystem's environment, such as by going out on the water in a rowboat.

24. The _____ found in freshwater draw their identity from the chemical balance peculiar to freshwater.

25. _____ also can be studied in forests and deserts.

26. His _____ on the breeding habit of micro-organisms and the impact of commercial boating is always standing-room-only.

27. A wide variety of _____ life can be found in wetlands.

28. Seeing for yourself how the wetlands are shrinking is an _____ experience.

29. Most of the human impact of the past half century has been _____, as wetland areas shrink each year.

30. The level of _____ felt by environmentalists is warranted, when you take into consideration the rate at which the rain forest is being destroyed.

Answer Key

1. any form of life
2. troubling
3. bad
4. effect
5. awareness-raising
6. misleading
7. striking
8. an integrated community of living organisms
9. material characteristics
10. to give form to
11. living in or near the water
12. group that interacts with another in a specific area
13. speech
14. to take part in
15. to live in
16. shapes
17. deceptive
18. impact
19. community
20. inhabit
21. physical
22. impressive
23. to participate
24. organisms
25. ecosystems
26. lecture
27. aquatic
28. eye-opening
29. negative
30. distress

11 Economics I

Match each word or phrase to its meaning:

1. to register	to provide with a job	
2. advanced degree	money deriving from one's labor or investment	
3. agency	to have an impact on	
4. loan	management or government procedures	
5. to employ	part of the academic year	
6. price	a belief based on actions or thoughts	
7. consumer goods	to sign up for	
8. policy	established organization	
9. theory	amount that something costs	
10. to relate	government bureau	
11. overall	to have a connection with	
12. institution	beyond the undergraduate level	
13. semester	with everything taken into account	
14. to affect	money advanced at interest	
15. income	materials that directly satisfy human wants	

Can you figure out the meanings of the italicized words in the following passages?

Conversation One:

CHARLIE: I'm really enjoying my economics class.

ROB: Maybe you should take the second part of the class next *semester,* when the professor focuses on recent government *policy* and its relationship to the *pricing* of *consumer goods.*

CHARLIE: I've already *registered* for it.

Conversation Two:

ROB: Would you want to work in a bank?

CHARLIE: Once I get an *advanced degree* in business, I want to work in an *agency* that aids developing countries.

ROB: Sitting in an office at an agency sounds boring. Would you make *loans?*

CHARLIE: Exactly. That way I could be part of helping different economies. Frankly, I don't think it would be boring at all.

Short Talk:

Money makes the world go round. The economy *affects* the level of national *income,* how many people are *employed,* and *prices* for *consumer goods,* as well as the banking system and fiscal *policy.* The study of economics looks at money *theories* and how they *relate* to *institutions* and to the *overall* behavior of the economy.

Fill in the blanks to complete the sentences:

16. To get money for school, he applied for a large _____.

17. The _____ set for goods affect how many people can consume them.

18. The new company will _____ dozens of people in our area.

19. An indication of economic health is the amount of _____ purchased.

20. The economic _____ set by the federal government eventually affects everyone.

21. Academic _____ on stimulating a healthy economy are adopted by policy makers.

22. The amount of money people spend is usually _____ to how much they earn.

23. After school, she moved to Washington, D.C., where there are numerous federal _____.

24. Economists can be interested in following the overall _____ of the economy as it responds to different trends.

25. Lending _____ and their rates can affect consumer behavior.

26. To get a space in the class, you have to _____ ahead of time.

27. The academic year is divided into _____.

28. A national crisis can _____ the economy.

29. He went to graduate school to earn an _____ in his chosen field.

30. Because of the robust economy, personal _____ has increased.

Answer Key

1. to sign up for
2. degree beyond the undergraduate level
3. government bureau
4. money advanced at interest
5. to provide with a job
6. amount that something costs
7. materials that directly satisfy human wants
8. management or government procedures
9. a belief based on actions or thoughts
10. to have a connection with
11. with everything taken into account
12. established organization
13. part of the academic year
14. to have an impact on
15. money deriving from one's labor or investment

16. loan
17. prices
18. employ
19. consumer goods
20. policy
21. theories
22. related
23. agencies
24. behavior
25. institutions
26. register
27. semesters
28. affect
29. advanced degree
30. income

Match each word or phrase to its meaning:

1.	paramount	wide scope
2.	mutual	area
3.	to manage	important
4.	position	to receive as a return for effort
5.	to enter	positive
6.	breadth	to be the overall director of
7.	to earn	to form into a coherent unit
8.	activity	concept of exchanging goods and services
9.	field	of greatest importance
10.	to organize	to do well
11.	beneficial	job
12.	to stimulate	to make something grow
13.	critical	affecting both parties
14.	market	a pursuit
15.	to succeed	go into

(handwritten note next to item 6: "anchur? amplitud")

Can you figure out the meanings of the italicized words in the following passages?

Conversation One:

SAM: Economics has a *paramount* role in our society.

REBECCA: I don't think it is more *critical* than any other field.

SAM: I disagree. Economics can help us understand why there aren't enough jobs available, and I'd say that that is an area of *mutual* concern to us.

Conversation Two:

CHRISTINA: I've accepted a job working for a company that *manages* new products.

SAM: Congratulations! What will you do in your new *position*?

CHRISTINA: I'll be providing services to businesses *entering* the *market* for the first time.

SAM: Sounds like you'll need considerable *breadth* of knowledge to *succeed*.

Short Talk:

Adults spend much of their lives *earning* a living. Economists study this behavior to learn how our institutions and laws affect people's economic *activities* and discover new and *beneficial* ways of *organizing* the country's *production* and consumption activities. Economics may sound dry, but most students find it *stimulating*.

Fill in the blanks to complete the sentences:

16. Her first _____ was as lending officer, but she was soon promoted to a new job at the bank.

17. Lending institutions and consumers getting loans have a _____ interest in the health of the economy.

18. Economics encompasses a _____ of topics, from environmental economics to economics of developing nations.

19. In the university setting, the economics curriculum is _____ to allow students to pursue their personal interests after they have completed a core of classes.

20. How people earn a living and spend their money is of _____ importance to economists.

21. The new agency gives out small loans that _____ the development of small businesses.

22. Analytical skills are _____ for success as an economics major.

23. Economists analyze a number of factors related to price before their corporations _____ new products onto the market.

24. Creating products and consuming them are two large-scale _____ that interest economists.

25. Economics is a _____ of study that helps people in such careers as government, business, banking, and the foreign service.

26. Launching that fantastic new project will no doubt be _____ to the company's finances.

27. Studying how a new product finds its way into the _____ can be a good research project for an economics class.

28. Being good with money is critical to _____ in the business world.

29. Most people must _____ their living in order to survive.

30. After getting his degree in economics, he went on to _____ a branch of an investment firm.

Answer Key

1. of greatest importance
2. affecting both parties
3. to be the overall director of
4. job
5. to go into
6. wide scope
7. to receive as a return for effort
8. pursuit
9. area
10. to form into a coherent unit
11. positive
12. to make something grow
13. important
14. concept of exchanging goods and services
15. to do well

16. position
17. mutual
18. breadth
19. organized
20. paramount
21. stimulate
22. critical
23. enter
24. activities
25. field
26. beneficial
27. market
28. succeeding
29. earn
30. manage

Match each word or phrase to its meaning:

1. extensive	4 to tell the meaning of
2. to focus	9 to keep equal in proportion
3. critical	6 to meet
4. to interpret	10 to last
5. genre	8 distinguishing structure
6. to encounter	11 authoritative list of books
7. context	3 involving careful judgment
8. form	12 something that might be attained
9. to balance	5 category characterized by a particular style or form
10. to endure	13 new
11. canon	1 considerable
12. horizon	14 not part of the majority culture
13. fresh	7 interrelated conditions in which meaning exists
14. minority	15 to widen
15. to broaden	2 to center one's attention

Can you figure out the meanings of the italicized words in the following passages?

Conversation One:

MAURICE: I'm late for the poetry reading.

DEBBIE: Isn't the poet someone who was in our anthology this semester?

MAURICE: Yes, and he won that award. Readings by award-winning writers make the texts easier to *interpret*.

Conversation Two:

MAURICE: The department is having a long discussion about what they teach us. There's some disagreement about whether there are enough writers from different cultures represented in the *canon*.

DEBBIE: I would like to *focus* on more women authors.

Short Talk:

English department classes focus on the *extensive* body of writing in the English language. Classes *focus* on the works themselves, as well as on *critical* reading, *interpretation* of texts, and the nature of literary *genres*. Students *encounter* recent developments in theory and traditional practices of close reading. Some texts are studied as aesthetic objects, and others are studied in relation to their social, intellectual, and historical *contexts*. Literature classes examine all the major literary *forms*. The field of English seeks to *balance* a respect for an *enduring* commitment to the traditional *canon* of literature and an expanding *horizon* of *fresh* concerns brought on by *minority* writers and a *broadening* of ways of looking at literature.

Fill in the blanks to complete the sentences:

16. Current discussion is leaning towards of expanding the _canon_ to incorporate new writers.

17. The specific _genre_ of literature that is in great demand today is postcolonial writing.

18. Great new writers are constantly on the _horizon_, waiting for recognition.

19. Classics are works whose meaning and enjoyment has _endured_ for readers throughout the centuries.

20. The _context_ of the play could change, depending on the perspective with which you read it.

21. Of the major _forms_, the short story is my favorite.

22. Departments are being forced to _balance_ teaching traditional works with incorporating new voices.

23. Taking literature classes will _broaden_ your appreciation of reading.

24. For his senior seminar, he chose _to focus_ exclusively on Shakespeare's history plays.

25. Studying the great writers trains you to read with a _critical_ eye.

26. The department voted to allow some _fresh_ texts to join the reading list.

27. _minority_ and other disenfranchised voices are beginning to be heard in the canons of English departments.

28. Students will _encounter_ contemporary ways of analyzing texts.

29. She was able _interpret_ centuries-old texts through a contemporary context.

30. With such an _extensive_ array of choices in the catalog, it is difficult to choose only a few courses.

Answer Key

1. considerable
2. to center one's attention
3. involving careful judgment
4. to tell the meaning of
5. category characterized by a particular style or form
6. to meet
7. interrelated conditions in which meaning exists
8. distinguishing structure
9. to keep equal in proportion
10. to last
11. authoritative list of books
12. something that might be attained
13. new
14. not part of the majority culture
15. to widen

16. canon
17. genre
18. horizon
19. endured
20. context
21. forms
22. balance
23. broaden
24. to focus
25. critical
26. fresh
27. minority
28. encounter
29. to interpret
30. extensive

14 Environment

Match each word or phrase to its meaning:

1. innovative — dangerous chemicals
2. absorbing — to engage as a participant
3. regulations — to include as a topic
4. to recognize — to exercise authority
5. to involve — interesting
6. concern — general survey
7. to cover — to acknowledge
8. to pollute — to inspire someone to do something
9. to contaminate — to contaminate or make unclean
10. hazardous waste — something done in a new way
11. overview — outline
12. framework — marked interest
13. to govern — recent happenings in the news
14. to motivate — authoritative codes for performing something
15. current events — to infect by association

Can you figure out the meanings of the italicized words in the following passages?

Conversation One:

STELLA: That was a great hike in the country.

STANLEY: I thought that visit to the recycling facility was a good idea.

STELLA: Seeing *innovative* uses for old products is interesting. And recycling also helps to save the environment.

Conversation Two:

STELLA: I've been attending some *absorbing* lectures about environmental policy.

STANLEY: Tell me more about them.

STELLA: So far, the instructor has been talking about water *regulations*. They're really important in the struggle to prevent *contamination* of the environment through the dumping of *hazardous wastes*.

Short Talk:

There is a growing *recognition* that the environment is in danger, and many young people are actively *involved* in environmental issues. The environment can be damaged intentionally or inadvertently. Courses *concerned* with the environment cover air and water *pollution*, *contaminants* like *hazardous wastes*, and other factors that affect marine, plant, and human health. Classes usually give an *overview* of the legal and regulatory *framework* that *governs* these issues. Many students are *motivated* by *current events* affecting the environment.

Fill in the blanks to complete the sentences:

16. The teacher is dynamic, which makes the class _____.

17. Each state _____ the process by which people can propose legislation to protect the environment.

18. _____ the problem with pollution, the government enacted the Clean Water Act.

19. Getting _____ in caring for the environment, for example by joining a clean-up crew, is a good idea.

20. An introductory class will give you a brief _____ of subject matter you might study in detail later.

21. Factories are prevented from dispersing toxic, _____ _____ into the air or water.

22. Each state varies in its environmental laws, but the organizing _____ is set up by the federal government.

23. _____ over rampant pollution created environmental regulations.

24. A class in environmental studies will _____ the history of the environmental movement, plus case studies of regulations.

25. _____ spoils the air and water for all of us.

26. Environmental problems are _____ often in the news.

27. A toxic spill from a factory can _____ the water downstream.

28. The landfill operators took an _____ approach that no one had tried before.

29. The government keeps pollution in check by _____ factory waste.

30. A strong desire to protect the earth _____ people to learn about the environment.

Answer Key

1. something done in a new way
2. interesting
3. authoritative codes for performing something
4. to acknowledge
5. to engage as a participant
6. marked interest
7. to include as a topic
8. to contaminate or make unclean
9. to infect by association
10. dangerous chemicals
11. general survey
12. outline
13. to exercise authority
14. to inspire someone to do something
15. recent happenings in the news
16. absorbing
17. governs
18. recognizing
19. involved
20. overview
21. hazardous waste
22. framework
23. concern
24. cover
25. pollution
26. current events
27. contaminate
28. innovative
29. regulating
30. motivates

15 Film

Match each word or phrase to its meaning:

1. to enroll   state of being
2. amusing   admiration of values
3. work   to subject to detailed thought
4. to analyze   very deep
5. mediocre   a distinct group of enterprises
6. industry   to develop
7. existence   to register for a class or program
8. fledgling   to make known
9. profound   mode of artistic expression
10. medium   of moderate quality or ability
11. to evolve   advanced system of practical
                      knowledge
12. technology   entertaining
13. appreciation   representation of a story
14. to reveal   new, recently born
15. narrative   the product of energy

Can you figure out the meanings of the italicized words in the following passages?

Conversation One:

WANDA: I'm taking a film *appreciation* class. We meet at a movie theater.

RONALD: That sounds like fun. How do I *enroll*?

WANDA: You can sign up for next semester soon.

Conversation Two:

WANDA: Studying film is more than just an *amusing* way to pass an evening. It's amazingly complex.

RONALD: I can't imagine that the typical action film would be all that complex.

WANDA: You'd be surprised. Though I must admit that we do concentrate on the *works* of the major directors. We *analyze* them to see how the shots were made.

RONALD: At least you'll be able to tell a good film from a *mediocre* film.

Short Talk:

Film is both an art form and an *industry*. While film has been in *existence* for only about a century, making it a *fledgling* art form in comparison to books or paintings, the *medium* has already profoundly affected our culture. The medium of film continually *evolves*, as the *technology* used to make it expands. By taking a film class, you can gain a deeper *appreciation* of what a film *reveals*. By studying different approaches to film, students will acquire an understanding of the *narrative* and visual styles that films employ.

Fill in the blanks to complete the sentences:

16. Before you can attend class, you first _____ by signing up.

17. While films may be _____, they also reveal serious aspects of our culture.

18. Films can be _____ of art, just like paintings or books.

19. By carefully _____ the shots, students can learn how the mind of the director worked.

20. Very few films can be classified as great art; most are _____.

21. The film _____ employs thousands of people in different jobs.

22. It's hard to believe that films have been in _____ for only about a hundred years.

23. At the beginning of the century, film was a _____ art and industry.

24. Film has had a _____ impact on how we spend our leisure time.

25. Film is an art _____ many people find especially accessible.

26. Film has continued _____ and reflect changes in society.

27. The _____ used to make film has been greatly changed with computers.

28. A class can teach you to look critically at a film and have a deeper _____ of it.

29. Films often _____ how cultures see themselves.

30. The _____ strategy in film is revealed in visual terms and not just through language.

Answer Key

1. to register for a class or program
2. entertaining
3. the product of energy
4. to subject to detailed thought
5. of moderate quality or ability
6. a distinct group of enterprises
7. state of being
8. new, recently born
9. very deep
10. mode of artistic expression
11. to develop
12. advanced system of practical knowledge
13. admiration of values
14. to make known
15. representation of a story

16. enroll
17. amusing
18. works
19. analyzing
20. mediocre
21. industry
22. existence
23. fledgling
24. profound
25. medium
26. to evolve
27. technology
28. appreciation
29. reveal
30. narrative

Match each word or phrase to its meaning:

1. to monitor	consequences
2. backbone	to closely examine
3. to showcase	importance
4. location	urban, relating to a city
5. significance	to take up a place
6. implications	having common racial, national, or cultural bonds
7. to occupy	innumerable
8. spatial	to keep track of
9. property	to include within a scope
10. to comprise	a position or site
11. myriad	trait peculiar to a person or thing
12. climate	long-standing condition of weather
13. to investigate	essential feature
14. metropolitan	relating to the extent of space
15. ethnic	to demonstrate visibly

Can you figure out the meanings of the italicized words in the following passages?

Conversation One:

STUART: Our new professor was recently on a project overseas.

CINDY: I heard he was *monitoring* El Niño.

Conversation Two:

CINDY: The department's archives have a splendid collection of maps.

STUART: I'm not surprised. Maps form the *backbone* of geography, because they *showcase* of lot of information.

CINDY: I can't imagine making a map where none existed before.

Short Talk:

Geography is the study of *location* and place. It is based on three fundamental questions: Where are things located? Why are they located where they are? And what is the *significance* or *implications* of the location of things? These "things" can be both human and physical phenomena that *occupy* places which have *spatial properties* or characteristics. More specifically, geography is both a social and a natural science *comprised* of a *myriad* of different subdisciplines whose topics are many and diverse. Physical geographers, for instance, study *climates*, soil, and land forms. Human geographers will concentrate on the features resulting from people's activities and characteristics. They may *investigate* overpopulation in *metropolitan* areas, territorial disputes, trade between countries, or the *ethnic* makeup of a neighborhood.

Fill in the blanks to complete the sentences:

16. Geographers look for visual ways to _____ and visually reference geographic information.

17. Geographers are interested in the physical and human _____ of space.

18. There are a _____ of things a map could describe, but a focus is necessary so that the map is legible.

19. The _____ of satellite images is clear and is conveyed every time the television uses an image.

20. The map showed _____ characteristics on the land, but the graph showed the impact of time.

21. Geography is _____ of many distinct interest groups.

22. The _____ of the research center was clearly marked on the map.

23. The map dealt with physical information only, so it was unable to demonstrate the _____ of new housing in the county.

24. People everywhere depend upon the accurate _____ of weather trends in order to plan their activities.

25. The bizarre weather recently warrants further _____ by scientists.

26. A map can be used to illustrate the _____ or racial distribution of people in a given area.

27. Geographers will investigate any potential _____ changes from major environmental disruptions.

28. Social geographers will document the changes in neighborhoods as a _____ area ages.

29. One of the essential _____ of the ocean is that it is huge.

30. Certain tools, like maps, form the _____ of any journey into an unfamiliar area.

Answer Key

1. to keep track of
2. essential feature
3. to demonstrate visibly
4. a position or site
5. importance
6. consequences
7. to take up a place
8. relating to the extent of space
9. trait peculiar to a person or thing
10. to include within a scope
11. innumerable
12. long-standing condition of weather
13. to closely examine
14. urban, relating to a city
15. having common racial, national, or cultural bonds

16. showcase
17. occupation
18. myriad
19. significance
20. spatial
21. comprised
22. location
23. implications
24. monitoring
25. investigation
26. ethnic
27. climate
28. metropolitan
29. properties
30. backbone

17 History

Match each word or phrase to its meaning:

1. introductory   of great service
2. exception   to add value to
3. resource   of profound thought
4. to document   make possible
5. primary   facet
6. to enrich *enriquecer*   to come face-to-face with
7. to enable *permitir*   stock of information
8. society   noteworthy
9. to confront   to record through evidence
10. valuable   defined range
11. aspect   beginner level
12. period   to stress
13. intellectual   communities of people
14. remarkable   special allowance
15. to emphasize   first hand

Can you figure out the meanings of the italicized words in the following passages?

Conversation One:

MILLIE: I'd like to take an upper-level class in American history this semester, but the department requires completion of the *introductory* class first.

RANDY: Maybe the department will make an *exception* in your case.

MILLIE: I hope so. The professor is here for only one semester.

Conversation Two:

RANDY: My history research project is coming along well.

MILLIE: What's your topic?

RANDY: I am using the local historical society's *resources* to *document* the unique political movement in this area during the last century.

MILLIE: It must be challenging to use *primary* research methods.

Short Talk:

The study of history *enriches* the intellect and the imagination. By revealing the human past in its *remarkable* complexity, history *enables* people to understand their own *society* and to think in an informed way about the great issues still *confronting* us. History's *emphasis* on research and writing is *valuable* no matter what career one chooses. Courses cover all *aspects* of history from different time *periods* and different continents. History is not just the study of politics, but also of social and *intellectual* issues.

Fill in the blanks to complete the sentences:

16. Students make use of _____ found in libraries, historical societies, and oral histories.

17. History has begun _____ the stories of minority cultures as well as dominant cultures.

18. His favorite _____ of history is the opening of the American west.

19. Knowing more about the past will _____ and benefit our experience of the present.

20. Our combined _____ is the product of its past.

21. His _____ research allowed him to work with antique letters from a special collection.

22. Learning about the past in detail forces people to _____ unfounded opinions.

23. The analytic skills obtained through research and writing are _____ later in life.

24. The range of human experience that history covers is _____.

25. If there is a good reason, departments can sometimes make an _____ to their policies.

26. Not all the different _____ of history make civilization look good.

27. History students learn _____ their research with careful notes.

28. _____ history is concerned with how ideas were transmitted through time.

29. Usually one completes the _____ class before taking an advanced class.

30. Knowing the methods of historians will _____ students to do well later in graduate school.

Success with Words for the TOEFL

Answer Key

1. beginner level
2. special allowance
3. stock of information
4. to record through evidence
5. first hand
6. to add value to
7. to make possible
8. communities of people
9. to come face-to-face with
10. of great service
11. facet
12. defined range
13. of profound thought
14. noteworthy
15. to stress
16. resources
17. to emphasize
18. period
19. enrich
20. society
21. primary
22. confront
23. valuable
24. remarkable
25. exception
26. aspects
27. to document
28. intellectual
29. introductory
30. enable

18 Horticulture

Match each word or phrase to its meaning:

1.	to thrive	a necessity
2.	variety	to ascertain the nature of something
3.	to operate	to include
4.	to collect	strong
5.	to categorize	unbelievable
6.	characteristics	to gather or accumulate
7.	requirement	individual traits
8.	to cultivate	an abundance of knowledge
9.	to encompass	fragile, requiring care
10.	wealth	to grow well and quickly
11.	taxonomy	assortment
12.	incredible	to classify into groups
13.	to identify	classification in an ordered system
14.	delicate	to perform a function
15.	vigorous	to grow or tend a plant

Can you figure out the meanings of the italicized words in the following passages?

Conversation One:

JENNY: Our class is taking a *field trip* to the Botanical Gardens.

MATT: You must be learning about an *incredible variety* of trees and vines.

JENNY: Not only that, we're also learning how a greenhouse *operates.*

Conversation Two:

MATT: I've *collected* more than 50 types of plants.

JENNY: First we need *to identify* the plants. Then we can *categorize* them by their *characteristics.*

MATT: My assignment is to talk about the different *requirements* needed *to cultivate* plants in nature.

Short Talk:

Horticulture classes provide a *wealth* of knowledge about plants and their uses. Horticulture *encompasses* botany, *taxonomy*, plant diseases, soils, and gardening techniques. Horticulturists learn about the *incredible* variety of plants—from *delicate* flowers to *vigorous* trees. They often find work in greenhouses in botanical gardens. If you take horticulture classes in different seasons, you will see different plant materials in bloom. Sensitive, tropical plants like orchids require heat and humidity, while hardy fir trees are able to *thrive* in cold, wintry conditions.

Fill in the blanks to complete the sentences:

16. Plants have adapted to their environment by branching out into a _____ of different types.

17. Because of the earth's different climates, soils, and other growing conditions, there is an _____ variety of plant material.

18. Many plants can be _____ just by looking at them.

19. Plants are divided into different _____ depending on their family and uses.

20. Plant _____ such as size and shape determine how they are categorized.

21. Trees are slow-growing but _____ plants that resist many diseases.

22. She _____ tomatoes the size of melons in her back yard.

23. The wide variety of plant types from different parts of the world provides a _____ of interesting material.

24. Plants are classified by the principles of _____.

25. A horticulturist might go on _____ a greenhouse or other setting where plants are the focus.

26. In a greenhouse, people can cultivate plants that need special conditions in order to _____.

27. Most horticulture classes require students _____ plant samples so they can examine a wide range of actual plants.

28. All plants _____ sunlight, water, and soil material in order to grow.

29. Some plants are _____, and live for just a few hours.

30. The study of plants _____ a range of growing conditions and diseases.

Answer Key

1. to grow well and quickly
2. assortment
3. to perform a function
4. to gather or accumulate
5. to classify into groups
6. individual traits
7. a necessity
8. to grow or tend a plant
9. to include
10. an abundance
11. classification in an ordered system
12. unbelievable
13. to ascertain the nature of something
14. fragile, requiring care
15. strong

16. variety
17. incredible
18. identified
19. categories
20. characteristics
21. vigorous
22. cultivated
23. wealth
24. taxonomy
25. to operate
26. thrive
27. to collect
28. require
29. delicate
30. encompasses

19 Landscape

Match each word or phrase to its meaning:

1.	returning student	monetary assessment
2.	career	related to business
3.	hobby	following the authority of
4.	commercial	place
5.	to observe	to divert attention
6.	site	student returning to college after spending time in the workforce
7.	tools	affecting the total calendar year
8.	according to	relating to the five senses
9.	aesthetic	relaxation pursuit
10.	year-round	to flower
11.	sensory	to look at
12.	value	related to beauty
13.	to distract	serving as an illustration or example
14.	to bloom *florece*	work experience
15.	sample	implements

Can you figure out the meanings of the italicized words in the following passages?

Conversation One:

YVETTE: I need to draw a plan based on a real *site* for my land-scape design class. I'd like to use your property as a *sample* of what I can do.

BILL: That's fine with me.

Conversation Two:

YVETTE: It was so cold yesterday. Why would you want to walk around outside in the winter?

BILL: I was surprised to see how much more attention I paid to the shape of the branches and the texture of the bark of trees when I was not *distracted* by the leaves and *blooms*.

YVETTE: The plants do look very architectural at the moment.

Short Talk:

In a landscape design class, you might meet other students from your university or older *returning students* who are preparing for a second *career*. Landscape design classes are excellent preparation for a career in the field or to pursue as a self-enriching *hobby*. Landscapers use design principles to improve the appearance of a home or *commercial* site. Students will learn new ways of *observing* the site and will use plants as their *tools*. Students discuss plants *according* to their use in the design, their association in nature, and their interesting characteristics. They aim to create an *aesthetic* plan, to provide *year-round* interest, to increase the *sensory* impression of the site, and to increase the *value* of the property.

Fill in the blanks to complete the sentences:

16. Even _____ sites for banks or law offices will benefit from some landscaping.

17. There is personal enjoyment and property _____ associated with keeping the yard of your home in beautiful shape.

18. Most of the benefits of landscape design relate to the visual _____ of the garden.

19. Designing with plants helps your _____ develop into the most beautiful it can be.

20. _____ real estate agents, good plantings can help a house sell faster.

21. Once spring is here, shrubs will begin to _____.

22. She used her neighbor's lot as a _____ site for her first design project.

23. Plants and structures are the _____ that a landscape designer uses.

24. Landscape design is a popular class with _____, who are reevaluating what they want to do with their lives.

25. A screen of trees or climbing plants can _____ one from an ugly view.

26. Design exposure and plant identification requirements train the eye to see more when you _____ a site.

27. Landscape design classes can start a career or be a pleasant _____.

28. Many clients have a _____ interest in their properties and enjoy bringing plants into bloom throughout the seasons.

29. Those who choose landscape design as a _____ need to be aware that they might have to do a lot of work outdoors.

30. The _____ pleasures of walking through a well-landscaped garden can be considerable—all five senses may be stimulated.

Answer Key

1. student returning to college after spending time in the workforce
2. work experience
3. relaxation pursuit
4. related to business
5. to look at
6. place
7. implements
8. following the authority of
9. related to beauty
10. affecting the total calendar year
11. relating to the five senses
12. monetary assessment
13. to divert attention
14. to flower
15. serving as an illustration or example
16. commercial
17. value
18. aesthetics
19. site
20. according to
21. bloom
22. sample
23. tools
24. returning
25. distract
26. observe
27. hobby
28. year-round
29. career
30. sensory

20 Math

Match each word or phrase to its meaning:

1. to struggle *luchr* to strive to reach
2. astute discourse intended to persuade
3. command to set in a valid order
4. endeavor dealing with the principles of
   ezluer zo /intentn validity
5. to revolve distinct
6. structure shrewd
7. logical to see
8. to compute to center around
9. argument to determine by mathematical
   means
10. proof component
11. problem attempt, activity
12. to construct question raised for inquiry and
    solution
13. clear arranged in a definite pattern
14. to view control over something
15. branch that which induces validity
    diversifcorse

Can you figure out the meanings of the italicized words in the following passages?

Conversation One:

DARRELL: I'm *struggling* with these math problems. I just can't seem to *construct* this last *proof*!

LOUISE: Maybe you just haven't learned to think in a *logical* manner, unlike me. I solved one from an academic journal last night.

DARRELL: Well, that's great for you—but I'll be up all night at this rate.

Conversation Two:

LOUISE: What kinds of jobs do math majors go into?

DARRELL: Some teach math in schools and others go into professional jobs that rely on an *astute command* of number theory.

LOUISE: I'm worried about not getting a good job.

DARRELL: Relax! All our graduates do well in their *endeavors*.

Short Talk:

Mathematics classes *revolve* around the *structures* of numbers. Courses emphasize *logical* relations and *computational* procedures. They provide experience in reading and writing mathematical *arguments* and serve as an introduction to *proofs* and number *problem* solving. Students will learn to *construct* proofs and to write them *clearly*. Mathematics professors usually *view* computing as a *branch* of mathematics.

Fill in the blanks to complete the sentences:

16. Whatever _____ she goes into, whether it is teaching or research, I know she'll succeed.

17. The class teaches the _____ of number groups.

18. Every April, Americans _____ their income taxes.

19. Geometry is based on memorizing various _____.

20. His interests _____ around computer applications.

21. She has a strong _____ of the material, and her confidence shows.

22. He _____ a sophisticated proof to advance the number theory he had developed.

23. He _____ with calculus, and then he dropped the class.

24. With his _____ knowledge of math, George was able to teach his colleagues how numbers could be used in a business setting.

25. The department chair _____ computing as a component of the math department.

26. Being able to write a proof _____ is the hallmark of a good mathematician.

27. Mathematics stresses _____ relations between numbers and among number groups.

28. Mathematics examples, often called _____, are challenging to solve.

29. Computing began as a _____ of the discipline of mathematics.

30. She was able to refute the _____ described in the mathematics journal.

Answer Key

1. to strive to reach
2. shrewd
3. control over something
4. attempt, activity
5. to center around
6. arranged in a definite pattern
7. dealing with the principles of validity
8. to determine by mathematical means
9. discourse intended to persuade
10. that which induces validity
11. question raised for inquiry and solution
12. to set in a valid order
13. distinct
14. to see
15. component

16. endeavor
17. structure
18. compute
19. proofs
20. revolve
21. command
22. constructed
23. struggled
24. astute
25. views
26. clearly
27. logical
28. problems
29. branch
30. argument

21 Music

Match each word or phrase to its meaning:

1. mandatory   to present
2. recital   to endure
3. to offer   required knowledge or coursework
4. survey   recurrent behavior
5. to waive   periods of time characterized by specific events
6. prerequisite   overview
7. integral   required
8. eras   to have effect upon
9. to remain   to relinquish
10. to pursue   to strive or accomplish
11. talent   styles
12. trends   public performance of music
13. to influence   a marked, innate artistic ability
14. discipline   comprehensive study
15. habit   essential or necessary for completeness

Can you figure out the meanings of the italicized words in the following passages?

Conversation One:

WILBUR: Are you going to the concert tonight?

FRANCES: Attendance is *mandatory* for my music history class.

WILBUR: I hope it's as good as that *recital* last month.

Conversation Two:

FRANCES: The department is *offering* a special class on women in music next semester.

WILBUR: I can't wait to sign up. Is it a *survey* class?

FRANCES: It's an advanced class, but they are *waiving* the prerequisite.

WILBUR: I wonder if they will cover any popular styles, or just classical styles.

Short Talk:

Music is an *integral* part of any person's education. People who study music have a better understanding of the history and culture of different *eras*, and have an appreciation for the power and beauty of music that will *remain* with them for a lifetime. If you play an instrument, a music course can help you to *pursue* a career in music or improve your skills so that you can better enjoy your *talents*. If you don't play an instrument, music classes can help you learn more about the *trends* that *influence* what you hear. The *discipline* gained by studying music theory and from the practice of an instrument will build good *habits* for the future.

Fill in the blanks to complete the sentences:

16. Music from the big band _____ is back in style.

17. Her musical _____ may be inspired by her equally gifted family.

18. Daily practice is a good _____ if you play an instrument.

19. The department's course _____ change each semester.

20. Because she knew a lot about the period of music, the department _____ the required class.

21. Daily practice is usually _____ when you are learning to play an instrument.

22. Your enjoyment of music will _____ long after college is over.

23. Knowing about music has been considered _____ to the development of a cultured person.

24. Small concerts, such as _____, often feature only a few performers.

25. Music history classes help students to discern the different _____ that have influenced music.

26. As with other art forms, historical happenings have _____ and changed music.

27. The _____ she gained by practicing the cello every day helped her later in law school.

28. He wishes he had _____ his music studies instead of switching to business.

29. The required course is a _____ of the role of music in western society.

30. The introductory class is a _____ for the advanced class.

Answer Key

1. required
2. public performance of music
3. to present
4. overview
5. to relinquish
6. required knowledge or coursework
7. essential or necessary for completeness
8. periods of time characterized by specific events
9. to endure
10. to strive or accomplish
11. a marked, innate artistic ability
12. styles
13. to have effect upon
14. comprehensive study
15. recurrent behavior
16. era
17. talent
18. habit
19. offerings
20. waived
21. mandatory
22. remain
23. integral
24. recitals
25. trends
26. influenced
27. discipline
28. pursued
29. survey
30. prerequisite

22 Philosophy

Match each word or phrase to its meaning:

1. traditional   basic essence of something
2. cornerstone   to be uncertain in a belief
3. to search   foundation
4. nature   to investigate a new area
5. leeway   relating to principles of right and wrong
6. to probe   able to move by argument
7. to doubt   to look for
8. grounding   to penetrate
9. to explore   significance
10. meaning   longstanding
11. basis   training in a fundamental field of knowledge
12. morality   accumulated learning
13. bioethics   margin or variation
14. wisdom   moral implications in medicine
15. persuasive   basic element

Can you figure out the meanings of the italicized words in the following passages?

Conversation One:

CAROLYN: I saw you coming out of the hospital. Are you okay?

TIM: Yes. My philosophy paper is on medical *bioethics;* I was talking with a counselor at the hospital.

CAROLYN: It must take a lot of *wisdom* to do that job.

Conversation Two:

TIM: The purpose of this introductory class in philosophy is to discuss the great questions of all time and the most *persuasive* answers to those questions.

CAROLYN: Philosophy isn't relevant to my life.

TIM: Philosophy is related to all aspects of contemporary life. It deals with the *meaning* of life itself.

CAROLYN: I can't help *doubting* that.

Short Talk:

Philosophy is one of the *traditional* courses of study and the *cornerstone* of a university education. It asks some difficult and *searching* questions about human existence and the *nature* of the universe. Philosophy gives the mind the greatest possible *leeway* to *probe* and *doubt*. In addition to developing a *grounding* in thinking skills, students *explore* questions about the *meaning* of life and the *basis* of *morality*.

Fill in the blanks to complete the sentences:

16. The _____ of good and bad personal decisions can be examined through the study of philosophy.

17. Philosophy is a good _____ for further studies in the law or medicine.

18. Studies in philosophy allow people _____ and find the basis of our beliefs.

19. Philosophy examines the essence or _____ of the principles we hold to be true.

20. _____ is especially concerned with the impact of contemporary technology on humans.

21. _____ an issue until you find its very essence is the hallmark of philosophy.

22. The exploration of age-old questions may give students the _____ to make good decisions with their lives.

23. Philosophy is flexible enough to deal with _____ topics as well as current topics.

24. Philosophy has asked all the questions relevant to mankind's _____ for meaning.

25. The _____ of our decision making in law may be found in a long tradition of studies in philosophy.

26. The most _____ arguments in ancient philosophy have been remembered and handed down to our era.

27. _____ whether the material world really exists is a passion only a philosopher would accept.

28. The _____ to doubt or criticize has influenced philosophical thought.

29. Many people need to feel they understand the _____ of life in order to gain a sense of happiness and security.

30. Because of its importance in culture, philosophy is a _____ of an advanced education.

Answer Key

1. longstanding
2. basic element
3. to look for
4. basic essence of something
5. margin or variation
6. to penetrate
7. to be uncertain in a belief
8. training in a fundamental field of knowledge
9. to investigate a new area
10. significance
11. foundation
12. relating to principles of right and wrong
13. moral implications in medicine
14. accumulated learning
15. able to move by argument

16. morality
17. grounding
18. to explore
19. nature
20. bioethics
21. probing
22. wisdom
23. traditional
24. search
25. basis
26. persuasive
27. doubting
28. leeway
29. meaning
30. cornerstone

23 Physics

Match each word or phrase to its meaning:

1. journal		to use
2. relevant		to make known for the first time
3. domain		next to
4. to discover		when two entities engage with one another
5. laws		difficult
6. motion		applying to everyone
7. interaction		to take meaning from something unsaid
8. to apply		magazine with scholarly articles
9. universal		harsh
10. to cluster		sphere of influence
11. to infer		to group together
12. challenging		action or function
13. alongside		meaningful
14. rigorous		skill
15. dexterity		rules

Can you figure out the meanings of the italicized words in the following passages?

Conversation One:

LAKEISHA: Our class experiments this summer will focus on the *laws* of physics and the environment.

BRADLEY: My project is on radon gas in buildings.

LAKEISHA: You'll have to start your research by reading studies in scientific *journals.*

Conversation Two:

BRADLEY: Have you heard about the new telescope at the observatory?

LAKEISHA: My astronomy class is using it tomorrow. We are studying the evolution of the stars.

BRADLEY: Is the "Big Bang" theory still *relevant?*

LAKEISHA: It's too early in the semester for me to tell.

Short Talk:

The *domain* of physics is all forms of matter and energy. Physics seeks to *discover* the *laws* that govern *motions* of material objects and waves, and the *interactions* between particles. *Applying* these *universal* laws to systems ranging from atoms and molecules to *clusters* of galaxies gives rise to *challenging* problems whose solution requires insight *alongside* logical *rigor* and mathematical *dexterity.* The study of physics helps teach the scientific method and its implications. It teaches how to make rational *inferences* from data and how to test hypotheses critically. Physics is related to other areas of knowledge and their technological applications.

Fill in the blanks to complete the sentences:

16. Applying _____ laws to local phenomena makes physics more interesting.

17. Scientists seek to _____ new information about the extinction of dinosaurs.

18. The _____ of magnetic fields is of tremendous interest to physicists.

19. During class, students learn to _____ principles to common phenomena.

20. Astronomers are particularly interested in how stars gather into _____.

21. Mathematicians working _____ physicists have developed many of the principles of physics.

22. College libraries subscribe to _____ published by academic societies.

23. The scientific method teaches students to make reasonable _____ from what is observable.

24. Quantum physics continues to _____ existing perceptions of space and time.

25. Organizing the physics curriculum is the _____ of the department chair.

26. The _____ of gravity governs our daily lives.

27. Classical mechanics is an aspect of physics that is concerned with _____ and inertia.

28. The intellectual _____ of physics demands a command a mathematics and a knowledge of chemistry.

29. Journals publish research _____ to many experimental projects.

30. The _____ of her mind allows her to nimbly jump from physics to mathematics to music.

Success with Words for the TOEFL

Answer Key

1. magazine with scholarly articles
2. meaningful
3. sphere of influence
4. to make known for the first time
5. rules
6. action or function
7. when two entities engage with one another
8. to use
9. applying to everyone
10. to group together
11. to take meaning from something unsaid
12. difficult
13. next to
14. harsh
15. skill

16. universal
17. discover
18. interaction
19. apply
20. clusters
21. alongside
22. journals
23. inferences
24. challenge
25. domain
26. law
27. motion
28. rigor
29. relevant
30. dexterity

24 Politics

Match each word or phrase to its meaning:

1.	candidate	to enlighten intellectually
2.	issues	short meeting to give essential information
3.	to nominate	customary beliefs related to a national or ethnic group
4.	briefing	academic offerings
5.	compromise	to clear up
6.	force	settlement marked by mutual concessions
7.	contemporary	group having the power of effective action
8.	curriculum	someone who runs for office
9.	to illuminate	essential character
10.	body	to gain
11.	to resolve	modern, current
12.	to attain *realize*	group of persons
13.	to incorporate	matters of interest
14.	identity	to unite with something already existing
15.	cultural	to propose someone for an office

Can you figure out the meanings of the italicized words in the following passages?

Conversation One:

BART: Our class project is to track press coverage of one *candidate* throughout the election.

SHANA: That's a good way to study this year's presidential election.

BART: I'll be able to see how the national *issues* affect my candidate's campaign.

Conversation Two:

SHANA: I've been *nominated* for an internship at the United Nations. I'll be attending *briefings* related to food security problems in developing nations.

DENISE: What a great opportunity! That should help you get a job in the foreign service after you graduate.

Short Talk:

Politics has been called the "art of the *compromise.*" How do political *forces* mesh to bring about changes? Political science provides an understanding of the political forces and institutions that affect *contemporary* society. The *curriculum* also *illuminates* the ways that governing *bodies* from around the world and throughout history have tried to *resolve* conflicting demands, *attain* and retain power, and respond to the problems of the societies they serve. Political science classes *incorporate* information relating to economics, social welfare, national *identity*, and *cultural* issues.

Fill in the blanks to complete the sentences:

16. _____ by the contributing sides has provided for some of the United States' most visionary political principles.

17. In the United States, the national parties _____ a presidential candidate at a special convention.

18. Laws, such as the U.S. tax code, often reflect _____ issues as well, such as social welfare programs.

19. The political science _____ at your university is sure to cover national and international issues and political theory.

20. A close study of the rules by which such governing bodies as the parliament operate _____ some of their seemingly arcane ways of behavior.

21. The power of a _____ of government like Congress is delegated to federal agencies like the Environmental Protection Agency.

22. _____ the problems of society at large while dealing with demands within their parties can keep politicians busy.

23. When a candidate seeks to become the U.S. president, he or she tries to _____ the highest elected seat in the nation.

24. For political parties to survive, they have to _____ different elements and appeal to a broad segment of the population.

25. Political _____ clash daily because of opposing ideologies.

26. How and why one of many _____ becomes the national leader is fascinating to scholars and the general public.

27. _____ politics is the product of historical elements in politics and other cultural forces.

28. The press corps reports on the daily _____ by government officials regarding current legislation and national events.

29. While we like to complain about our political system, our sense of national _____ springs from our political system.

30. Politicians debate the _____ of the day, many of them dealing with the economy and social welfare.

Answer Key

1. someone who runs for office
2. matters of interest
3. to propose someone for an office
4. short meeting to give essential information
5. settlement marked by mutual concessions
6. group having the power of effective action
7. modern, current
8. academic offerings
9. to enlighten intellectually
10. group of persons
11. to clear up
12. to gain
13. to unite with something already existing
14. essential character
15. customary beliefs related to a national or ethnic group

16. compromise
17. nominate
18. cultural
19. curriculum
20. illuminates
21. body
22. resolving
23. attain
24. incorporate
25. forces
26. candidates
27. contemporary
28. briefings
29. identity
30. issues

25 Psychology

Match each word or phrase to its meaning:

1. to approve	to formulate
2. memory	afraid
3. to permit	to stick to
4. to design	understanding
5. background	intense
6. individual	to be aware of
7. to perceive	in the not too distant past
8. apprehensive	to give consent
9. to adhere	able to be determined in advance
10. predictable	period of time that one lives
11. recent	to enable
12. subsequent	following close after
13. keen	to assess
14. life span	the ability to remember
15. to measure	a single person

Can you figure out the meanings of the italicized words in the following passages?

Conversation One:

LESLIE: My internship was *approved*. I'll be doing a clinical semester at a treatment center for substance abusers.

EILEEN: Are you *apprehensive* about working with them?

LESLIE: No, I think it will be a great learning experience.

Conversation Two:

EILEEN: This semester, the class will meet twice a week in the cognitive and human performance lab.

LESLIE: Is this where we investigate human *memory*?

EILEEN: Yes. The lab is equipped with computer work stations that will *permit* you to see how humans perform.

LESLIE: I'd like to *incorporate* biofeedback into this work.

Short Talk:

A degree in psychology is *designed* to provide a strong *background* in the biobehavioral sciences. Psychology is interested in everything relating to the *individual* and how that person *perceives* him or her self. Normal development, while individuated, does *adhere* to some stages that are *predictable*. Of *recent* interest are theories related to how biology affects the development of the brain, and the *subsequent* impact on personal identity. Traditionally, psychology students have also been *keenly* interested in how the personality develops over the *life span*. The ways that children learn, as well as tests and other *measurement* devices and how they are developed, are another area of long-standing interest.

Fill in the blanks to complete the sentences:

16. _____ breakthroughs in genetics have altered some of the arguments surrounding inherited and acquired behaviors.

17. The heart rate and skin temperature monitors _____ the class to see the effect of the interrogation on the subject.

18. The role of the _____ as he adjusts to the demands of the larger society is the hallmark of psychology.

19. He was _____ about meeting with the psychotic, dangerous patient.

20. Many of the observations were subjective, but the evaluation did _____ to the guiding principles of normal child development.

21. Before he could take the senior seminar, the department chair had to give her _____.

22. One of the cornerstones of psychology is evaluating different tools _____ the learning capacity of children.

23. The doctor started him on a new drug and his delusions _____ diminished.

24. Adolescent angst, which seems so personalized, is a _____ stage of life.

25. His _____ in psychology was useful when he went into the criminal justice system.

26. The impact of diseases like Alzheimer's has made the public anxious for more knowledge on the function of _____.

27. Psychologists are _____ interested in the breakthroughs in molecular biology and their effects on development of the brain.

28. Human development is an ongoing journey that continues over the entire _____.

29. He _____ a maze for the rat to follow in order to find the dish of pellets.

30. At some time, we all _____ our own behavior differently than others observe it.

Answer Key

1. to give consent
2. the ability to remember
3. to enable
4. to formulate
5. understanding
6. a single person
7. to be aware of
8. afraid
9. to stick to
10. able to be determined in advance
11. in the not-too-distant past
12. following close after
13. intense
14. period of time that one lives
15. to assess
16. recent
17. permitted
18. individual
19. apprehensive
20. adhere
21. approval
22. to measure
23. subsequently
24. predictable
25. background
26. memory
27. keenly
28. life span
29. designed
30. perceive

26 Religion

Match each word or phrase to its meaning:

1.	empathy	writings
2.	symbol	not immediately obvious
3.	allusion	to speak out
4.	subtle	imprecise
5.	to anticipate	to inspect
6.	vague	aspect
7.	attention	reference
8.	to express	established form for a ceremony
9.	to examine	close observation
10.	to voice	contrary to
11.	dimension	understanding for another person
12.	to favor	to state
13.	against	to wait for
14.	text	something that stands for something else
15.	ritual	to like better

Can you figure out the meanings of the italicized words in the following passages?

Conversation One:

DON: Why are you taking a class in eastern religion?

FREDDIE: I want to have more *empathy* for people of different cultures.

DON: Oh, that sounds really interesting!

Conversation Two:

FREDDIE: I'm an art history major, but I need to take a religion class to understand the religious *symbols* used in art.

DON: Some of those visual *allusions* are *subtle*.

FREDDIE: I hadn't *anticipated* how many religious stories are used in painting.

DON: My memory of those religious stories is *vague*.

Short Talk:

The study of religion focuses *attention* on the role faith plays in the lives of individuals and societies. Religion classes provide a context for understanding ourselves and our belief systems. They respect religious concepts and practices as *expressions* of faith and *examine* them in that context. A variety of perspectives will be *voiced*. Students will study the basic concepts of many religious traditions, such as Christianity, Judaism, Islam, Buddhism, and Hinduism. While students will engage in the study the spiritual dimension of reality, most departments take no position in *favor* of or *against* religions. The goal is to see how religious *texts*, symbols, and *rituals* constitute communities.

Fill in the blanks to complete the sentences:

16. Religious _____ have influenced other pieces of writing.

17. The department does not promote religious experiences, so it does not take a stand for or _____ current religious issues.

18. The distinctions between certain religious arguments are so _____ as to be almost nonexistent.

19. People have long used faith to _____ their perception of reality.

20. She did not _____ how many pieces of classical music are settings of religious texts.

21. Anthropologists find religious _____ to be an illuminating window into a culture's traditions.

22. The department did not take a stand in _____ of or against the religious debate.

23. Religious studies pay _____ to the role of faith in people's lives.

24. By _____ our own concepts of morality, we can see how we have been influenced by religious traditions.

25. By studying cultures we know little about, we can develop _____ for them.

26. Departments seldom _____ an opinion on a politically charged area of religious debate.

27. Developing the spiritual _____ of our lives can enrich us.

28. If you stop reading the ancient stories, your memory of their content can get _____.

29. The painting makes a visual _____ to an ancient story from the Old Testament.

30. Her research is focused on the recurrent use of the _____ of the moon in various cultures.

Answer Key

1. understanding for another person
2. something that stands for something else
3. reference
4. not immediately obvious
5. to wait for
6. imprecise
7. close observation
8. to state
9. to inspect
10. to speak out
11. aspect
12. to like better
13. contrary to
14. writings
15. established form for a ceremony
16. texts
17. against
18. subtle
19. express
20. anticipate
21. rituals
22. favor
23. attention
24. examining
25. empathy
26. voice
27. dimensions
28. vague
29. allusion
30. symbol

Match each word or phrase to its meaning:

1.	setting	to discover, to have the opinion that
2.	seasoned	to satisfy
3.	integrated	period of life from birth to about one year of age
4.	condition	typical manner in which one reacts to certain things
5.	bureaucracy	to understand the true worth of
6.	to find	unified, interrelated
7.	behavior	widely, across all countries
8.	exceptional	variety
9.	diversity	contextual environment
10.	to fulfill	well-being
11.	welfare	out of the ordinary
12.	to qualify	circumstance
13.	global	to be eligible for, based on competency
14.	to appreciate	experienced
15.	infancy	system of government administration

Can you figure out the meanings of the italicized words in the following passages?

Conversation One:

WAYNE: I'll be working in a community *setting* all year.

DOMINIQUE: That's a great way to get experience in the field, working with *seasoned* professionals.

Conversation Two:

DOMINIQUE: My trip to Latin America was great. We looked at the remains of some ancient irrigation system.

WAYNE: I don't see why that was so fascinating.

DOMINIQUE: Well, now I can *appreciate* the significance of all the water symbols in art work found in digs.

Short Talk:

Sociology is the study of human interaction, and sociologists study the ways in which people live together under various social and cultural *conditions*. As the world becomes more *globally integrated*, a better understanding of the human condition becomes essential. Sociology looks at the ways in which people affect each other in all aspects of their lives, from *infancy* through old age, in families, among friends, and under great *bureaucracies*. Sociology graduates have *found* that a better understanding of human *behavior* is *exceptionally* useful in any kind of employment. Anthropology, a related subject, studies the *diversity* of human cultures. Some sociology students are *fulfilled* by the thought of a career in social service aiding in people's social *welfare*. *Qualified* students may obtain internships in which they are supervised by professionals.

Fill in the blanks to complete the sentences:

16. Sociologists are interested in the ways in which people _____, such as when two families are joined through a marriage.

17. Anthropology has established the _____ of human cultures throughout history.

18. There are only a few open slots for the internship, so only the most _____ applicants will be considered.

19. An _____ of the diversity of human nature is essential to the well-educated person.

20. Students will _____ that opportunities to learn more about human interaction are readily available in a sociology class.

21. Social service agencies are charged with ensuring the safety and _____ of persons at risk.

22. Working in a community _____ is one way to get career direction.

23. A huge _____ covers laws and regulations relating to employment, education, discrimination, and social welfare.

24. The new anthropology course features the _____ impact of television across cultures.

25. People live under different _____ depending on the region in which they live, their age, their class, and their interests.

26. Many students take one or two sociology classes to better understand what influences the _____ they see exhibited by people.

27. Many students decide to undertake a major in sociology because they find the idea of a career in social services to be _____.

28. Even in _____, when children are most connected to their mothers, they are also affected by other family members.

29. Her supervisor had 20 years of experience, and was considered by all to be a _____ professional.

30. Understanding why people behave in a certain way is of _____ benefit at work and at home.

Answer Key

1. contextual environment
2. experienced
3. unified, interrelated
4. circumstance
5. system of government administration
6. to discover, to have the opinion that
7. typical manner in which one reacts to certain things
8. out of the ordinary
9. variety
10. to satisfy
11. well-being
12. to be eligible for, based on competency
13. widely, across all countries
14. to understand the true worth of
15. period of life from birth to about one year of age
16. integrate
17. diversity
18. qualified
19. appreciation
20. find
21. welfare
22. setting
23. bureaucracy
24. global
25. conditions
26. behavior
27. fulfilling
28. infancy
29. seasoned
30. exceptional

Match each word or phrase to its meaning:

1.	to practice	to pay the costs for
2.	technique	chance
3.	to persuade	tense, anxious
4.	to sponsor	to assess
5.	to eliminate	feedback that promotes improvement
6.	to coach	to become more precise
7.	to evaluate	faith in one's own abilities
8.	nervous	body of technical methods
9.	self-confidence	to inspect carefully
10.	to deliver	to remove
11.	to scrutinize	to give something
12.	constructive criticism	to perform repeatedly
13.	opportunity	to be more forceful
14.	to sharpen	to convince
15.	to strengthen	to train someone intensively

Can you figure out the meanings of the italicized words in the following passages?

Conversation One:

OLIVER: I overheard you *practicing*. Are you taking a singing class?

VERA: No, I'm taking a speech class. We are learning breathing *techniques*.

OLIVER: I guess that would make your voice stronger.

Conversation Two:

VERA: I want to be a more *persuasive* speaker, so my job is *sponsoring* me for this class.

OLIVER: What do you hope to get out of the class?

VERA: I am trying to *eliminate* my accent.

OLIVER: Maybe the teacher can *coach* you and *evaluate* your progress.

Short Talk:

Most people are *nervous* about speaking in public. A class can give you practice in public speaking and help you to develop the *self-confidence* you lack. A teacher can *scrutinize* your strengths and weaknesses. During a class, you will have an *opportunity* to speak, and the teacher and the other students will give you *constructive criticism* about your presentation. Everyone can benefit from *sharpening* his diction and *strengthening* his voice.

Fill in the blanks to complete the sentences:

16. _____ a speech repeatedly before a group is a good way to overcome your anxiety.

17. Soft voices can be helped with vocal _____ used by singers.

18. A voice can be made to sound more confident and hence more _____; remember, nervous speakers are generally not very convincing.

19. Often, employers _____ staff for public speaking classes.

20. Vocal coaching can _____ or reduce a regional accent.

21. A teacher can work closely with a student to _____ her on an individual basis.

22. Tapes can allow students to hear their own voices and _____ their progress.

23. She was so _____ about speaking in public that she began to sweat profusely.

24. Learning good skills usually builds _____ and makes it easier to perform well.

25. Once you _____ a speech to the class, you can relax.

26. A good teacher can _____ a student's performance and give detailed feedback.

27. You can count on other class members for _____ _____ that is sympathetic and helps you grow.

28. If your employer gives you an _____ to take a class, avail yourself of it.

29. You can _____ the precision of your diction and be more clear.

30. A class can make a soft voice sound more _____.

Answer Key

1. to perform repeatedly
2. body of technical methods
3. to convince
4. to pay the costs for
5. to remove
6. to train someone intensively
7. to assess
8. tense, anxious
9. faith in one's own abilities
10. to give something
11. to inspect carefully
12. feedback that promotes improvement
13. chance
14. to become more precise
15. to be more forceful
16. practicing
17. techniques
18. persuasive
19. sponsor
20. eliminate
21. coach
22. evaluate
23. nervous
24. self-confidence
25. deliver
26. scrutinize
27. constructive criticism
28. opportunity
29. sharpen
30. strengthened

29 Study Abroad

Match each word or phrase to its meaning:

1. culture shock — 15 to confuse
2. to translate — 6 student who is studying in a foreign country
3. residence permit — 2 to turn into another language
4. credits — 11 enough
5. funds — 10 paperwork
6. guest student — 3 permission to live in a country
7. tuition and fees — 13 to misunderstand
8. to recommend — 1 difficulty in adjusting to a new culture
9. to stipulate — 4 points used towards a college degree
10. documentation — 5 money
11. sufficient — 14 country in which guest student lives
12. familiarity — 7 cost of attending a college or university
13. to misinterpret — 8 to advise
14. host country — 12 knowledge of someone or something
15. to disorient — 9 to make a demand

Can you figure out the meanings of the italicized words in the following passages?

Conversation One:

CHARLES: I've been thinking about spending a year in France as a *guest student.*

RACHEL: That sounds fun. How complicated will it be for you to get a *residence permit* there?

CHARLES: All you have to do is prove to the authorities that you have *sufficient funds* to cover all your expenses.

Conversation Two:

MAX: How is Charles enjoying his year in France?

RACHEL: He's having a terrible time! He didn't study enough French before he left, so he has to ask people to *translate* everything for him. And the customs there are so different from ours that he's suffering from severe *culture shock.*

Short Talk:

It is *recommended* that those who plan on studying abroad *familiarize* themselves with the language and culture of the *host country.* Otherwise, they are likely to *misinterpret* many things and to feel *disoriented* and unhappy. Immigration authorities also *stipulate* that guest students must provide *documentation* that they have *sufficient funds* to cover *tuition, fees,* and living expenses during their time in the host country. Finally, students should make sure they will be awarded *credits* at their home universities for the courses they take abroad.

Fill in the blanks to complete the sentences:

16. The bustling crowds shouting in a language that she didn't understand made Marcia feel _disoriented_ .

17. If you don't have a valid _resident permit_ for this country, you may be sent home by the authorities.

18. He had to ask the Arab man to _translate_ the document, since he had forgotten what little Arabic he knew.

19. _guest students_ broaden their horizons much more than students who stay at home.

20. If you don't pay _tuition & fees_, you cannot attend class.

21. She was given a residence permit as soon as she provided the _documentation_ the authorities required.

22. The more _familiarize_ you have with the customs of a country before you leave home, the more likely it is that you will not suffer from culture shock once you get there.

23. American universities sometimes refuse to give _credits_ for classes taken at foreign institutions.

24. I _recommended_ that you take a good Chinese-English dictionary with you on your trip to Shanghai.

25. Many study-abroad programs _stipulate_ that students be fluent in the language of the host country.

26. You've studied five years of Swahili; that should be more than _sufficient_ for you to get by in Tanzania.

27. The shopkeeper _misinterpreted_ what she said and gave her an apple instead of the orange she had asked for.

28. Henry's _funds_ ran out and he couldn't afford to stay the entire year.

29. Surprisingly, you can get _culture shock_ when you return to your own country if you spend a long time abroad.

30. Guest students often spend a year studying in the _host country_.

Answer Key

1. difficulty in adjusting to a new culture
2. to turn into another language
3. permission to live in a country
4. points used towards a college degree
5. money
6. student who is studying in a foreign country
7. cost of attending a college or university
8. to advise
9. to make a demand
10. paperwork
11. enough
12. knowledge of someone or something
13. to misunderstand
14. country in which guest student lives
15. to confuse
16. disoriented
17. residence permit
18. translate
19. guest students
20. tuition and fees
21. documentation
22. familiarity
23. credits
24. recommend
25. stipulate
26. sufficient
27. misinterpreted
28. funds
29. culture shock
30. host country

30 Teaching

Match each word or phrase to its meaning:

1.	role	subject
2.	to retain	to adapt
3.	to simulate	to participate actively
4.	to augment	to remember
5.	topic	to provide an opportunity
6.	to excite	to speed up
7.	activity	a means of reaching something
8.	to allow	to create a representation of
9.	to experience	assembled group
10.	approach	to raise interest
11.	level	goal
12.	to accelerate	a part played for learning purposes
13.	to modify	degree
14.	audience	to improve
15.	objective	process to stimulate learning through participation

Can you figure out the meanings of the italicized words in the following passages?

Conversation One:

JILL: I am observing an elementary school teacher for my education class.

MARTIN: Does she have good teaching *approaches*?

JILL: She has the students do a lot of *role* playing. They *retain* more of the lesson that way.

Conversation Two:

JILL: The teacher created a game to *simulate* how insects pollinate plants.

MARTIN: Do the kids enjoy the involvement?

JILL: Yes, it really seems to *augment* their learning environment.

MARTIN: It's good for kids to be active and not always sitting at a desk.

Short Talk:

Good teachers make *topics* that might sound dull *exciting* to their students. Teachers often use *activities* that *allow* students to *experience* the course material, not just listen to it. This *approach* can bring a new *level* of involvement to students while *accelerating* their learning process. Students can play different roles in a lesson and engage in *simulations*. Teachers can *modify* a good lesson plan to suit the age of their *audience* while still maintaining the original learning *objectives* of the lesson.

Fill in the blanks to complete the sentences:

16. Lesson _____ give the teacher a method of evaluating success.

17. By _____ a situation, the students can engage in different roles.

18. The age and skills of the _____ determine which learning methods are most effective.

19. Some teachers believe experiential learning _____ the pace at which students learn new material.

20. Different _____ and subject matters lend themselves to simulations.

21. A teacher can combine traditional and experiential _____ to learning.

22. Experiential _____ diversify the ways students can learn.

23. Role playing is a good way _____ the lesson plan.

24. The classroom _____ is enlivened when students bring their ideas to their studies.

25. When students can play a _____ in a lesson, they are engaged in the story.

26. Teachers can _____ a lesson plan to different needs of their students.

27. Some experts say that experiential learning helps students _____ what they learn longer.

28. Students can become _____ and show their enthusiasm about a topic.

29. Activities and simulations _____ students to bring their own perspectives to the work.

30. Depending on the grade _____ of the students, the lesson objectives can be simple or complex.

Answer Key

1. a part played for learning purposes
2. to remember
3. to create a representation of
4. to improve
5. subject
6. to raise interest
7. process to stimulate learning through participation
8. to provide an opportunity
9. to participate actively
10. a means of reaching something
11. degree
12. to speed up
13. to adapt
14. assembled group
15. goal
16. objectives
17. simulating
18. audience
19. accelerates
20. topics
21. approaches
22. activities
23. to augment
24. experience
25. role
26. modify
27. retain
28. excited
29. allow
30. level

Index

to enroll	57	firm	1
to enter	45	fledgling	57
era	81	fluent	29
essential	29	to focus	49
ethnic	61	force	93
to evaluate	109	form	49
to evolve	57	foundation	33
to examine	101	framework	53
example	21	fresh	49
exception	65	to fulfill	105
exceptional	105	fundamental	1
to excite	117	funds	113
existence	57	to further	33
to experience	117	to gain	9
to experiment	17	genetics	5
expert	5	genre	49
to explore	85	global	105
to expose	13	to govern	53
to express	101	grounding	85
extensive	49	guest student	113
eye-opening	37	guidelines	29
familiarity	113	habit	81
to favor	101	hands-on	33
field	45	hazardous waste	53
financial	1	hobby	73
to find	105	horizon	49

manner	13	negative	37
market	45	nervous	109
material	13	to nominate	93
matter	17	objective	117
meaning	85	to observe	73
to measure	97	to occupy	61
mediocre	57	to offer	81
medium	57	to operate	69
memory	97	opportunity	109
message	25	organism	37
methods	13	to organize	45
metropolitan	61	original	21
minority	49	ornamental	5
minuscule	1	to outgrow	9
to misinterpret	113	overall	41
to modify	117	overview	53
to monitor	61	paradigm	25
morality	85	paramount	45
motion	89	to participate	37
to motivate	53	to perceive	97
movement	13	period	65
mutual	45	to permeate	25
myriad	61	to permit	97
narrative	57	to perpetuate	17
natural	17	to persuade	109
nature	85	persuasive	85

About

KAPLAN

Educational Centers

Kaplan Educational Centers is one of the nation's premier education companies, providing individuals with a full range of resources to achieve their educational and career goals. Kaplan, celebrating its 60th anniversary, is a wholly-owned subsidiary of The Washington Post Company.

TEST PREPARATION & ADMISSIONS

Kaplan's nationally-recognized test prep courses cover more than 20 standardized tests, including entrance exams for secondary school, college and graduate school as well as foreign language and professional licensing exams. In addition, Kaplan offers private tutoring and comprehensive, one-to-one admissions and application advice for students applying to graduate school.

SCORE! EDUCATIONAL CENTERS

SCORE! after-school learning centers help students in grades K-8 build academic skills, confidence and goal setting skills in a motivating, sport oriented environment. Kids use cutting-edge, interactive curriculum that continually assesses and adap to their academic needs and learning style. Enthusiastic Academic Coach serve as positive role models, creating a high-energy atmosphere whe learning is exciting and fun for kid With nearly 40 centers today, SCOR continues to open new centers nation wide.

KAPLAN LEARNING SERVICES

Kaplan Learning Services provic customized assessment, educat and training programs to K-12 scho universities and businesses to h students and employees reach th educational and career goals.

KAPLAN INTERNATIONAL

Kaplan serves international stude and professionals in the U.S. thro Access America, a series of inter English language programs, and

ernational Institute, a leading
provider of intensive English language
programs at on-campus centers in
California, Washington and New York.
Kaplan and LCP offer specialized
services to sponsors including place-
ment at top American universities,
scholarship management, academic
monitoring and reporting and financial
administration.

KAPLOAN

Students can get key information and
advice about educational loans for
college and graduate school through
KapLoan (Kaplan Student Loan Information Program). Through an affiliation
with one of the nation's largest student loan providers, KapLoan helps
direct students and their families
through the often bewildering financial
aid process.

KAPLAN PUBLISHING

Kaplan Books, a joint imprint with
Simon & Schuster, publishes books in
test preparation, admissions, education, career development and life skills;
Kaplan and *Newsweek* jointly publish
a highly successful guides, **How to
Get into College** and **How to Choose
a Career & Graduate School**. SCORE!
and *Newsweek* have teamed up to publish **How to Help Your Child Suceed
in School**.

Kaplan InterActive delivers award-winning high quality educational products

and services including Kaplan's
best-selling **Higher Score** test-prep
software and sites on the internet
(http://www.kaplan.com) and America Online. Kaplan and Cendant Software are jointly developing, marketing
and distributing educational software
for the kindergarten through twelfth
grade retail and school markets.

KAPLAN CAREER SERVICES

Kaplan helps students and graduates
find jobs through Kaplan Career Services, the leading provider of career
fairs in North America. The division
includes **Crimson & Brown Associ-
ates**, the nation's leading diversity
recruiting and publishing firm, and **The
Lendman Group and Career Expo**,
both of which help clients identify highly sought-after technical personnel and
sales and marketing professionals.

COMMUNITY OUTREACH

Kaplan provides educational resources
to thousands of financially disadvan-
taged students annually, working closely with educational institutions, not-for-
profit groups, government agencies
and other grass roots organizations on
a variety of national and local support
programs. Also, Kaplan centers enrich
local communities by employing high
school, college and graduate students,
creating valuable work experiences
for vast numbers of young people
each year.